Urban  For Beginners

Gardening For Beginners

Making Use Of Cramped Spaces And Growing Your Own Food For A Sustainable Living

By

Fhilcar Faunillan

Ⓒ Copyright 2015 by Content Arcade Publishing - All rights reserved.

This document is geared towards providing exact and reliable information in regards to the topic and issue covered. The publication is sold with the idea that the publisher is not required to render accounting, officially permitted, or otherwise, qualified services. If advice is necessary, legal or professional, a practiced individual in the profession should be ordered.

- From a Declaration of Principles which was accepted and approved equally by a Committee of the American Bar Association and a Committee of Publishers and Associations.

In no way is it legal to reproduce, duplicate, or transmit any part of this document in either electronic means or in printed format. Recording of this publication is strictly prohibited and any storage of this document is not allowed unless with written permission from the publisher. All rights reserved.

Urban Gardening For Beginners

The information provided herein is stated to be truthful and consistent, in that any liability, in terms of inattention or otherwise, by any usage or abuse of any policies, processes, or directions contained within is the solitary and utter responsibility of the recipient reader. Under no circumstances will any legal responsibility or blame be held against the publisher for any reparation, damages, or monetary loss due to the information herein, either directly or indirectly.

Respective authors own all copyrights not held by the publisher.

The information herein is offered for informational purposes solely, and is universal as so. The presentation of the information is without contract or any type of guarantee assurance.

The trademarks that are used are without any consent, and the publication of the trademark is without permission or backing by the trademark owner. All trademarks and brands within this book are for clarifying purposes only and are the owned by the owners themselves, not affiliated with this document.

Table of Contents

INTRODUCTION...................................7

Chapter 1 - Sustainable Living And Urban Gardening 101..........................12

Chapter 2 - How Urban Gardening Will Amp Up Your Life................................20

- Better Performance 21
- Leaving A Legacy 23
- Plants Are Happiness.......................25
- Health And Wellness 27
- Natural Pain-Reliever 30
- Beauty In A Natural Scenery 32
- Life-Saver And Giver 33

Chapter 3 - Self And House Preparations For An Urban Garden 34

Chapter 4 - Right Space, Right Place To Put Your Plants In 39

Chapter 5 - Plants: From Pots To Plates 58

Chapter 6 - Gardening TLC Lessons ..79

CONCLUSION 84

INTRODUCTION

I want to thank you and congratulate you for downloading the book, "Urban Gardening for Beginners: Making Use of Cramped Spaces and Growing Your Own Food for a Sustainable Living".

Have you ever turned on the television after a hard day's work, lounging on your bed or couch, and then you're just met with the news of dead people? Dead people who were victims of the conflicts in Middle Eastern countries or any other land under warfare. Or dead people from the famines in third world nations, like Africa. And more dead people from Mother Nature's wrath, such as super typhoon Haiyan in the Philippines and the earthquake which struck Nepal. Or people so unhappy about the current government system and economic crisis around the world. People losing jobs, houses, money left and right. People getting robbed, or shot, or bullied, or abused by other people. So, so many sad news around the world and all there's left for you to do is…turn off the TV.

It is an eye opener to think of so many things happening around you, do you care? Of course you do. But, is there anything you can do about it? That is the ultimate question, is there anything you *will* do? How do you solve all these problems? You're only one person, you can't possibly be the solution? Right? Wrong. People have underestimated the power of individual and simple solutions for so long. There are a lot of people out there who have big mouths spouting these big words, saying that they hold the answers in their grand schemes to save the world. But their big words do not automatically translate to big actions. Big mouths sometimes mean small hands.

It takes an individual to make a crowd, one person to start an initiative to change oneself and actually act on these problems rather than simply turning off the TV and talking about it. One of these initiatives is sustainable living. In this book, you will realize that you have the potential to change the world by changing the way you live your life, starting with learning how to grow your own food. You may be living in the city in a cramped apartment or you may not own a backyard or garden, everything is possible with a little creativity and this thing called Urban Gardening which enables you to have your own sanctuary at home and at the same time provide for your own needs.

With the world as it is today, it is time to make some concrete actions and help save the earth and its citizens. Let us not be selfish or disinterested. The world is not yet at an end, but the time we have left to live here can end at any moment. So, release all your creativity and resourcefulness and share it with the world. Use it for good through urban gardening where you can not only save yourself, but also Mother Nature herself.

Read this book and be enlightened by the simple solutions that you could use throughout your life. Learn how planting and learning how to live sustainably can make your life easier, happier, and stress free.

Thanks again for downloading this book, I hope you enjoy it!

Chapter 1 - Sustainable Living And Urban Gardening 101

Sustainable living is basically being environmentally, socially, and economically responsible. It is about making mindful and informed choices in every aspect of our life, with the goal of improving your quality of life and sustaining what is left of this planet for future generations.

Sustainable living may be construed as something akin to a hippie or going all out Amish, eating and using only organic or natural ingredients, getting rid of most of your belongings, probably grow your own farm, or giving up all the fun hobbies you used to do. But it's not that, living sustainably simply means that you are aware of the impact of the decisions that you make. Yes, it is a lifestyle choice but change does not happen in a day. It is an experiential and an ongoing process of learning and developing preexisting and new values.

Why? Why do we have to start changing the way we live our lives and the way we make our decisions? Why do I have to stop buying these products? Why do I need to take a break from my work? Why do I have to STOP?

Let's pause for a minute and answer these questions: do you remember what you did in the last few days? Or the things you bought? How about the people you talked to? Can you look five years into the future and know exactly where you want to be? Are you where you want to be right now? If you answered NO to any of these questions, then you've got an answer as to why you need a change, a fresh outlook in life, get a new perspective.

Today, we function on autopilot, we don't even know what we're doing. We are so manipulated by commercial products that we don't even realize it. Did you know that in the US alone the average households have over TEN THOUSAND POUNDS of material possessions? And that 43% families spend more than they earn. In the year 2013, Americans have consumed over 154, 000 pounds of Starbucks coffee, imagine the number of Starbucks cups were thrown with this magnitude of purchases.

Furthermore, we are overloaded by obligations and responsibilities, it's like we are digging our own graves with regrets and frustrations. We have stopped noticing the things that are happening right in front of us. It's time this is stopped. Nobody wants to live a life full of regrets and studies have shown that we regret more on the things that we DIDN'T do than on the things we did. If you list down the five things that you value the most right now, you might realize that you have not done a thing to show for your values and you might wonder if you value these at all. By living a sustainable life, you remove all these extras and actually work on what's truly important. Spend time with your family, go read what's on your book list, meet new friends, collect experiences and memories, plant your garden, and make your life worthwhile.

There are many ways to start living sustainably and one of the more popular, probably the most beneficial, and simplest ways to get you going towards a better you is through Urban Gardening.

Nowadays, the city-life, sky-rise infrastructures, malls, manufacturing companies are becoming more and more prominent in the rural areas and becoming more invasive to our mountains and almost every available land surface. These "developments" at the expense of cutting down trees, blocking river paths, drying up seas, generating pollutants, and intensifying climate change. Through all this, environmental activists and concerned citizens alike started the movement to create urban community gardens where people can come in and sow food producing plants to meet the demands for healthy food production.

Historically, urban gardening started as "allotment gardens" in Germany when food shortages and poverty were rampant. Then, this program boomed during the two world wars where survivors tilled "victory gardens" not only to assuage the need for food, but also for peaceful, social interactions.

It was in the 19th century, on World War I when the then American president, Woodrow Wilson, ordered that every empty plot be used for food production. Food shortages were rampant and they no longer had sufficient food supplies for their soldiers and other workers. Within 20 years, 5 million plots of land were cultivated and 500 million pounds of food were produced. This paved the way to the creation of the National Victory Garden Program from which programs were organized to have agricultural gardens within cities.

Poverty and emotional turmoil are just two of the natural consequences of war, but by gathering the community to cultivate their own land, sow herbs, fruits, and vegetables, and harvest them together, urban gardening has provided an avenue to gain some of their identity, a sense of belongingness, and independence back. Throughout history especially during the lowest points of humanity, planting brought the community together and kept people alive.

These historical events shaped the urban gardening movement that it is today. Today, urban agriculture is incorporated in several cities' plans and designs as an integration to policies geared towards building sustainable cities.

Not only did the urban agriculture movement pervade public policies, they are also permeating the private sector through the smaller urban gardens, which will be taught in the next chapters of this book. Now, food production has become a shared responsibility, dividing the bigger problems of food shortages and environmental damage chunk by chunk. For every person who engage in urban gardening and start producing their own food, the more people are fed and the lighter the burden to save mother earth. And with the increasing number of people becoming aware of this simple solution, sooner or later we won't have to deal with problems of unhealthy lifestyles, famine, malnutrition, climate change, and others.

Mr. Bill Gates himself, one of the world's richest men, declared that "investing in agriculture brings one of the highest returns you can have", and that it is indeed possible to feed the world if we can figure out how to do that without depleting our natural resources. By the end of this book, you will learn how to feed yourself and how to live a healthy lifestyle.

Chapter 2 - How Urban Gardening Will Amp Up Your Life

We all know that plants and gardening have positive effects to our lives, but to what extent you say? Well, basically in almost all aspects of your life plants make it better. In this chapter, you will learn some research and scientific findings on how plants have improved our way of life. Hopefully, this will encourage you to pursue urban gardening and influence other people to take on the habit as well.

Better Performance

Studies have shown that plants have a natural calming effect that facilitates concentration and memory. In one specific study, they attached electrodes to the participants' heads to monitor brain activity, physiological signs such as heart rates, sweating, and pulse rates were also monitored in the process. The results showed that when the participants touched a plant, the mental and physiological symptoms of stress and anxiety substantially reduced. Participants became calmer and more mindful.

In another study where two busy workplaces were compared, one with plant foliage and the other without any greeneries at all, it was found that there was lesser noise in the office with plants. People then worked better and were more focused at work, resulting to higher productivity. In the cities today, many offices and even some apartments, are windowless. Thus, these enclosed spaces conduct so much noise and distraction with no outlet, plants were able to abate these problems. Another beneficial result would be that office workers become less irritable and become more harmonious in working with other people.

Further evidence shows that nature or the presence of plants improve performance based on an experimental study whose results showed that participants who worked in an environmental condition had 20% better memory, performance, and accuracy in the given task compared to the participants who were placed in the normal workplace setting.

Plants are able to simulate your mind and the senses which helps in keeping up the energy and the brain capacity at top notch. However, for people who are constantly working or constantly busy or for people who have difficulty concentrating and remembering it can sometimes be difficult to access green spaces to be able to work. Parks are also not suitable to work on tasks, so the best option would be to make your own garden and reap all the mental, physical, and psychological benefits that plants can provide.

Leaving A Legacy

If we don't start changing our ways right now, then there is a very big chance that in the near future our children and grandchildren wouldn't even be able to experience nature. Trees may no longer exist in cities and all the animals they will see may only be from the zoo – most of them endangered or near extinction. By starting or learning how to plant in our own homes, we are educating the children on how to survive in the future. This is not something that they can simply learn inside the classrooms, planting is experiential and emotional. Through planting, you are raising a child with an advanced consciousness, a child who is aware, and a child who is grateful for the simple things in life.

This is another reason why people should always campaign for preserving and building green spaces, public botanical gardens, or vegetable patches in the community to foster responsibility among the citizens and the children. With the rapid acceleration of virtual communication, people are slowly disregarding personal connections, but these places can help bring the community together. In the confines of your home, gardening projects provide an avenue for the family to get together and actually do something together. For example, to celebrate a birthday or any achievement the family can plant a seed together as a symbol for reaching a goal, then you can all watch that plant grow together.

Plants Are Happiness

It is scientifically proven that plants generate happiness, reduce stress and symptoms of depression, and increase positive energy. Flowers, specifically, are proven to immediately improve one's mood. They can make you feel relaxed and secure. Evolutionarily, plants and flowers were mankind's allies. They provided us with food, shelter, protection from predators, and flowers symbolize that fruits are soon to appear and provide nutrition for the community. So, no matter how you say that you don't like flowers or think that it's too girly or cheesy, we are naturally inclined to like flowers.

Flowers make you have a better outlook in life and it's just one of those naturally beautiful things in the world without all the pretentions and alterations. So, if you want to make someone happy, whether a lover, friend, or a family member, flowers are definitely the way to go. But doing that could cost you substantially as flowers are surprisingly expensive. The solution? Plant your own flowers. Freshly picked flowers that you grew yourself definitely show more effort, sincerity, and a personal touch. Giving flowers this way is guaranteed to be better appreciated than store-bought ones.

Health And Wellness

Did you know that the pharmaceutical industry is one of the richest and fastest growing industry in the world? What with the promotion of unhealthy eating habits, sedentary lifestyles, pollution, stress, epidemic diseases, and many more disease-causing factors, it is no wonder that more and more at a younger age become chronically or terminally ill, enriching these pharmaceutical companies and economically sucking you dry.

It is a three-way problem with one simple solution.

Problem 1: Unhealthy diet. The food we eat today are either full of bad cholesterol or full of unnatural chemicals or both. Even when companies label their products as "natural", it is still not an assurance that you are not eating what you're not supposed to because the "natural" label may just be a marketing scheme used by companies to deceive customers into buying their products. Easily, if you grow your own food organically you know what goes into your system and you know that you're eating healthy. Understandably, you can't grow all food ingredients on your own, so you can buy certified organic food and they can be relatively more expensive than the mass-produced items, but you can reduce the cost by growing some of it on your own garden.

Problem 2: Sedentary lifestyle. More specifically, a sedentary lifestyle where you have close to nothing when it comes to exercise or any other physical activity. Around 60% of the world's population spend an average of 6 to 7 hours of sitting down and around 35% spend an average of 4 hours sitting down while watching television or spending time on the computer. United Kingdom's National

Health Service (NHS) linked sitting too much to various health issues such as obesity, hypertension, type II diabetes, certain kinds of cancer, and early mortality. Gardening help reduce your sitting down time everyday as you end to your plants. Ten minutes of physical exercise everyday is already a vast improvement from hours of sitting down doing nothing.

Problem 3: Outside health risk factors. Pollution, noise, and congestion are just three of the things that are outside of our control, but controls our mood and stress levels. They weaken the body's immune system, making you an easy target for germs and diseases. We already know how plants can mediate all of these outside influences. But you should know that the act of gardening is a scientifically proven outlet to drown out the stresses of life. With gardening, you can boost your self-reliance, feel more accomplished, and facilitate social interactions with others. When you have all that going on, you would be less bothered by what's happening outside, you become more mindful of what is salient and get rid of the distractions.

Natural Pain-Reliever

Plants do not only provide long-lasting effects on our well-being, but they have immediate effects as well. In a well-known study, two hospital patients who underwent an operation were sent to two different recovery rooms. The first one had plants in it while the second one was just a plain old hospital room. As expected, the patient in the plant room reported to feel less pain than the patient in the other room. Moreover, the first patient recovered faster than the second patient. Plants are also used in cancer and geriatric centers to help patients cope with their treatments both physically and emotionally. Through horticulture therapy, where they allowed the patients themselves to plant and care for their plants, patients recovered significantly faster than usual. If you have your own garden then you would spend less time turning to your medicine cabinet for aspirin or any other medication for that matter.

Mental health

If you have a family member, a friend, or anyone you know who might be suffering from mental disorders, you could suggest that they take up gardening. Gardening is often used as an experiential therapy especially for people with depression and anxiety mental illnesses. It promotes self-reliance and boost self-esteem that will improve how mentally-ill patients view themselves. People who went through a trauma are also encouraged to immerse themselves in nature. It was also found that children with attention deficit disorders cope better with plants around or in a natural setting.

Beauty In A Natural Scenery

People are often attracted to natural sceneries and symmetries and having plants in or around your home increases its attractiveness. A higher level of perceived attractiveness also increases perceived quality of life. Basically, having natural foliage in your home makes it look better and more expensive than it actually is. This also impacts the community positively in the sense that your home could be a model to making the community look aesthetically pleasing.

Life-Saver And Giver

No matter how we neglect our environment, it is an undeniable fact that we cannot live without plants. The world cannot exist without plants. Plants provide us with oxygen, clean air, food, and nutrition. Not to mention, plants protect us from calamities. Floods happen because we do not have trees and soil anymore to absorb the water from the rains.

Now that we have understood and appreciated the roles plants play in our lives, let us show our appreciation by preserving them and making our own gardens to lessen production that leads to more plants being cut down. Read on through the next chapter to get yourself started on making your own urban garden.

Chapter 3 - Self And House Preparations For An Urban Garden

Having your own garden with a bunch of little plants is like having a new baby come out of the ground. The birthing process and the caring methods may differ, but babies and plants both need a lot of TLC and commitment. Some of you may feel threatened by this because it might be a little too much commitment than you asked for, but don't worry it does not last forever. Like all children, they all flow out of the nest sometime only with plants it takes a very short time for them to mature enough for you to leave them alone.

Anyways, enough about babies and the birthing process. Let us get into planting!

First, you will need a cup of commitment. As mentioned before, gardening can take a lot of work but work that is worth it because it is so fulfilling at the end. Gardening is not just about planting the seeds and leaving it there, there are also a lot of maintenance that could go on depending on the plant itself and the season. There's weeding, watering, cleaning, and removing bugs and insects. These are just some of the stuff that you have to do. But, these are just small sacrifices that you have to make compared to the abundant list of benefits, provided in the previous chapter, on how plants will change your life for the better.

You could also look at this maintenance and extra hard work as exercise or your new exercise regime. Because that is the mission of urban gardening: promoting wellness in every aspect of your life.

Remove that image of perfectly manicured gardens you see in magazines and advertisements, because urban gardening will actually require *more creativity* than that. With the space you are working with and the type of environment you live in, it is important to harness all your creativity and resourcefulness inside to be able to make a conducive enough environment for your plants to grow. If you look around your space, you might get a little discouraged thinking that plants could not fit or actually grow there, but you are wrong. Plants are strong creatures that, with your assistance, could stand through any environment.

Hence, what you need to do is to look around your house or apartment again and see every empty space as a potential garden. To make choosing plants and preparing containers easier, try pre-conceptualizing where you are going to place your garden. Look through every nook and cranny, if you've identified space where you want to put in your plants, take the necessary measurements for that dimension. Taking measurements will give you a more realistic picture of how your garden would look like as well as make your life easier when you start setting up the containers and choosing the right size of plants.

Also, choose places where it is more conducive for plants, spots where the sun would shine through, where there is enough ventilation, where you could provide proper irrigation, and of course where you could weed properly without worrying so much about the mess. Once you've had this all worked out and you believe that you are ready for a change in your lifestyle, then read on to start setting up your first urban garden. You will lean in the following chapters, the different types of materials that you can buy or recycle for your containers, how to set these different types of containers to fit into your house or your balcony or your backyard, and then you can choose different types of plants that will suit your space and needs.

Chapter 4 - Right Space, Right Place To Put Your Plants In

When you live in an urban setting, having open large spaces, like a yard or a garden, is a luxury not many of us can afford. Thus, the emergence of urban gardening. Since you can't have the ground to plant your seeds in, you will have to utilize various containers to hold the soil and plants. Containers help utilize space and keep your garden organized.

So, this chapter will introduce you to several types of containers that you could use to pot your plants in. These materials could either be store-bought or, in keeping with the sustainable lifestyle you are starting, made up from recycled materials. You can also take on several DIY ideas that will be presented here so you can decorate your garden and make it your own.

These are the containers that will be described in this chapter along with instructions on how to use, place, and decorate them:

- Pots

- Raised beds

- Hanging baskets

- Other recyclable materials

Urban Gardening For Beginners

1. Pots

They are the most basic and common containers that you can find anywhere and they have a long, long range of sizes as well as materials used and colors. And these are just some of the things you have to consider if you use pots for some parts of your urban garden.

There are the usual orange red pots that we usually see, the terra cotta pot, then there is the waterproof glazed pots, then comes the wooden and plastic pots, and the latest innovations in the world of pottery are those made out of synthetic materials, like resin, fiberglass, and propylene, and even fabric pots. But if you don't have any of these pots available, you could always use an old bucket, they're basically look like pots anyways just drill some holes beneath them.

To make the right choice on certain types of pots that you could use, consider these three things: weight, porosity, and drainage.

Living in a cramped space, it is important to be able to move things quickly to get them out of the way or to create more space. Thus, it is important to choose the material that offers the greatest mobility. Any of the clay and wooden pots may not be the best option for you because most of them are heavy and then you have to factor in the weight of the soil and the plant itself. So, opt for smaller pots especially since you are still starting out so your plants are probably still on the smaller scale.

Next is porosity, porosity is the pot's property to allow air to circulate within the root system of the plant. This is important because oxygen is vital in the plant's photosynthesis, necessary for it to bear fruits and flowers. Porosity also gives the plant a chance to get rid of water excess and cooling down the soil. The more porous the container, the more easily the soil will dry out so you will have to water the plants more frequently too. Pots made of terra cotta, peat, and wood are some which have the most porosity.

Last but not the least is drainage. No matter what type of material you use, containers should always have a water drainage, most likely in the form of holes. And speaking of water, glazed pots, fiberglass pots, and fabric pots are waterproof, meaning they can last longer because they won't be damaged from moisture.

In addition, be careful when purchasing cheap plastic pots because they easily become brittle exposed to certain weather conditions, so you might just end up buying new ones every once in a while.

You may not buy new pots, you can reuse even the broken pots, if you have them. You can place some of the smaller plants in there and use the broken pieces as terraces to block the soil from overflowing. You can decorate it with old toys you have to create a simple landscapes look from single broken pot.

Also, if you want to save space on your spices, you can have a large pot and then arrange your rosemary, parsley, basil, green onions along the rim of the large pot. These spices can be cut or trimmed for harvesting easily so you would not have to worry about the plants overflowing the pot because you can pick them out easily. You can also incorporate wire meshes in the middle or around your pot to prepare for bigger fruit plants and some vines.

The easiest way to decorate a pot is to paint them, if you could find a weather resistant paint and something that is organic or made up of non-toxic materials to make sure that the plants don't get chemicals in them.

Pros: Highly available in the market, easy to set up, comes in different forms and sizes

Cons: Difficult to customize and limited when it comes to placement, they can be fragile, and they're relatively heavier.

Top spot for your pots: For the miniature plants in miniature pots, you can spread them around your house. On the ledge of your window, on any of your tables, and you can even hang them, especially with flowering plants. For the larger pots, you can place them beside your door, either outside or inside, that is after confirming the actual height your eventually grow into. So, for bigger plants you will prefer placing them outside, if you have any space, or in any of the empty corners of the room. Then, you can hang some of the smaller pots around the large pot or just simply set up the small ones around the big one.

2. Raised beds

Raised beds are often made by wood or lumber. This container is also widely available in the market, so you have two options: one is to buy a set either online or through your nearest gardening shop or two you can construct your own raised bed by using old refurbished wood or lumber slats you might have lying around or in a junk shop.

Raised beds are ideal for urban gardening because of the magnitude of pollutants present in the soil and the fact that there could actually be no soil around you enough for planting. The good thing about raised beds is that they are wonderful space savers. They may look big and intimidating, but they can hold a lot of plants in just one area of your space. You can also landscape it by having stacked raised beds, arranging your plants depending on growth size and yield.

They also provide good drainage system and it allows for deep rooting for your plants. If the root growth of your plants are stunted, it could mean that your plants would not bear any fruits. Also, wooden raised beds are weather or season-proof because the soil is not touching the ground you will have more control when it comes to the soil temperature. Lastly, raised beds can protect your plants from harmful worms and insects.

If you've decided to make your own raised bed, you will need the following materials:

- Lumber or wood: 2" x 4" or 6" or 8" planks, depending on how long you want it to be. More expensive wood have natural oils that would prevent from rotting. Pressure-tested wood are safe as they are certified to be safe for planting. Two-inch thick woods are optimal for planting because they would last longer against moist and other damaging conditions.

- Stakes: about 3 feet long, 1 to 2 inches in diameter, at least 4 pieces. These are necessary because these are what raise the wooden bed.

- Hammers

- Nails or screws

- Levelling device

So, the basic steps to building a pallet of any size are the following:

1. To make the edges, place two planks of wood side by side and fasten them with a smaller piece of wood at both ends. Using the exact same measurements, do this for the opposite side. The standard length for a wooden raised bed is four feet and the depth should be

no shorter than 12 inches deep for conducive root growth. Given that you probably only have a small space around your home to place your plants, it would be better to make the planter a bit narrower. So, for the two remaining sides stack the woods to the same height measurements as the first ones, but with make the length shorter this time.

2. Assemble the four pieces together with nails or screws to form a rectangle or square.

3. You may now place additional planks of wood across the corners to make the floor bed. Make sure to leave small gaps for ventilation and drainage.

DIY Idea: To create more space you would want to stack these boxes together. There are two ways to do this. First, is by creating a tall frame against a wall where you can attach your ready-made boxes to with nails or screws. This is ideal for small boxes and you can arrange the boxes asymmetrically for design purposes. Second, you can create a shelf with the boxes. You will still need a frame, but your beds should be longer. Also, if you really do not have that much wall space to work with, you can customize the shape of your box according to the dimensions of what available space you have. You can also create a trellis around your frames to contain the vines and bigger plants.

Pros: Customizable, have larger storage capacity, gives good drainage and plant protection

Cons: Vulnerable to rotting and weather conditions, difficult to place inside the house, challenging to construct

Top spot for raised beds: You can place these right outside your backdoor or you can place it right by your window as a plant box. It would definitely help improve your view.

3. Hanging containers

This is probably one you will enjoy the most making because it is very customizable, you have a lot of opportunity to design all you want, and it is also a very good activity to have with children. This is a big space saver because while you might not have a lot of leg room in your house, you can always utilize the head space. By hanging your containers and plants, you can also create a self-irrigating system that helps with saving water. The materials that you are going to use are recycled materials and the rest are things you could find at your basic arts and crafts store.

There are two most common materials you could use for your hanging garden and these are baskets and plastic bottles. For both materials, you have to make sure that they are lightweight enough that you could hang them and at the same time durable enough to hold your plants.

For baskets, you have to make sure that they have holes for drainage. These are very good for flowering plants or for fragrant herbs. Just imagine coming home every day to a fresh-smelling home from the herbs and flowers you have hanging around. Most commonly used baskets are the plastic ones and the traditional wire baskets which you can get from your local gardening shop.

Plastic bottles are much more customizable than the baskets and you also contribute a lot when it comes to protecting the environment from trash. You can make individual hanging bottles or you can have a sort of wall of plastic bottle of plant containers. Plastic bottles are only good for small herbs and plants, they are not healthy for shrubs.

You will need the following materials:

- Plastic bottles (at least 1.5 liters each)

- Cutter/scissors

- Nylon string or fishing string

- Washers

- Art materials (Colored pens and paints)

Here are the steps to hanging plastic bottle containers:

1. Place your bottle in a flat and empty table. If you want to have individual hanging bottles, place your bottle right side up. But if you want to stack them, place your bottle horizontally.

2. With your cutter, cut a square hole an inch from the bottle's neck all the way up to the middle of the body (for vertical bottles). For horizontal bottles, cut a larger hole 2 inches below the bottles neck all the way up to an inch from the bottom. The width should be about 2 to 3 inches.

3. Poke small holes along the sides of the bottle where the string will go through. And also poke holes on the bottoms of the bottles for drainage.

4. Pull the string through the small holes you poked and tie them with the washer to prevent them from moving or sliding. Leave a good 1 to 2 feet of space from the top of the string to the top of the bottle for hanging. For stacking bottles, repeat steps 1 to 3 for two more bottles and string them together.

5. Now, start decorating. You may ask your children to do this paint your bottles with any decorations you want. More popular

decorations are cute animal faces, especially for the vertical bottles. Or you could label each bottle decoratively with the name of your child or with the plant's name to make it educational and easy to identify when harvesting.

Top spot for hanging containers: The windows and at your front door are the best bets on where you can place your hanging containers. These containers are small enough that they don't look disturbing and messy, instead they look very cute. Or if you have a boring wall in your house, and you just don't have the energy to choose, buy, and glue a whole new wallpaper or you don't have the money to buy paintings or frames, design your walls with these plants instead.

Pros: Customizable, fun to create, simple and decorative, space saver

Cons: Not conducive for bigger plants and soil could easily dry out

4. Other recyclable materials

Practically any container large enough to hold plants and deep enough to contain its roots can be used for urban gardening. If you've browsed through the internet for some DIY ideas, you may have seen a lot of watering cans, old bathtubs, tires, or jars.

For seedlings, you can use jam jars to contain them. You can decorate these jars or wrap them up with decorative paper or some ribbons and line them up on your window sill. These are also a great idea for a gift for your other friends or family who wants to start their own gardens. You can place your younger plants here if you're still freeing up space from your house or if you think they are not yet ready for too much exposure.

As for tires, be careful with using recently manufactured ones because they contain chemicals that are not healthy for the soil and your plants. Ancient tires are good especially with their size, there is a lot of available space for you to get creative and landscape different plant species to make a small garden within the tire.

Old chairs and tables could be reused as shelving for your plants. Try gathering all the scrap materials you have in your house or garage and harness all your creative juices and get to planting.

Chapter 5 - Plants: From Pots To Plates

To live sustainably, you have to eat sustainably, not to mention healthily. Hence, the reason why growing your own food is so important these days with everything we consume coming from a manufacturing line of harmful chemicals that could cost us our lives. And think about how much money and time you are going to save by having your own food, in your own house! How great would it be when you're cooking and then you say, "Oh I need more tomatoes, no worries I'll just pluck some from my garden right here!" You can literally make your own "garden" salad. Get it?

The convenience and the sense of fulfillment is definitely unmatched. This chapter will help you fulfill those gardening fantasies of yours by identifying some of the basic herbs and vegetables that you can plant in your own garden along with nutritional facts, care requirements, amount of yield, and how to plant them. These are just some of the easier plants to grow with your beginner status, as you learn more about gardening and familiarize with other plant classifications, you may start planting more, like flowers and fruit trees which are a little trickier and more complicated.

If you are buying seeds from a gardening store and if it's your first time selecting plants, do not worry because they will have labels and details available for you about sizes. So, choose the seedlings labeled with "small" or "good for containers" or "miniatures" or "shrubs". And unless you really have enough space for it, you may choose the "jumbos" or "medium" seedlings. And if you are sticking with the healthy lifestyle, it would be great if you can get your hands on organic or heirloom seedlings. They may cost more but you would not be needing much anyway because you plants are gifts that keeps on giving so one seedling would already go a long way.

Moreover, the best way to grow herbs and vegetables is to group them according to their season. Some plants thrive with the cold and shrivel with the sun and some vice versa. It's important to take note on what seasons certain plants bloom so you don't waste your time and resources in maintaining them.

For hot season plants, these plants need warm soil to grow. The best time to plant these are at the end of the winter season and harvest at the end of spring or summer – depending on the plant's growth rate. If you already have them with you before you can plant them, then you might want to keep them indoors and placing them in non-porous containers, like plastic, to avoid drying the soil out. The same goes for cold season plants except in reverse seasonal order.

PLANTS THAT LIKE IT HOT

1. Peppers

Peppers are one of the healthiest foods that we eat, especially bell peppers. With a scientific name called, *Capsicum annuum,* these small and vibrant veggies provide you with 300% of Vitamin C. This will facilitate in iron absorption, provide you with antioxidants to fight against aging and energy deficiency. Peppers also burn a lot of calories and they prevent hypertension by having vitamin B6 and magnesium. They also contain lycopene, which is what gives them color, and what gives us protection from cancer cells. It is wonderful how one small vegetable can give you so much nutrition, make this veggie a part of your daily diet by having them around every day in your garden.

Unlike the cucumbers, peppers are slow growing so you may need to incubate the seeds indoors during spring time or purchase seedlings for transplants then take them out in the summer. Before you put in the seed, stick a stake in your pot or chosen container. The stake would help keep the plant upright and it should be about 3 to 4 feet tall. Or you could set up a frame or trellis to save more space.

If you chose compact varieties of peppers, you may be able to plant 2 to 3 seeds in a 14-inch container. Fill your container with your soil mix until about an inch from the rim. Dig about an inch to plant your seeds in, 5 at most to be thinned out later. Place the container where there will be direct sunlight and regularly water them. Fertilize plants once a week 2 to 3 weeks in from planting. Use organic and water soluble fertilizers as much as possible. Harvest the fruits of your labor once the pepper has ripened or fully colored. There are multiple varieties of peppers that you can use, from bell peppers to chili peppers. You can combine different colored species in one container to make an interesting garden.

2. **Tomatoes**

Tomatoes are ubiquitous, they are everywhere in the food that we eat.

They're in our pizzas, our condiments, our salads, soups, and pastas. Tomatoes are one of the most harvested vegetables all over the world. But if you prefer your sauces to be home made and not filled with chemical flavoring, it's best to make your own by growing your own tomatoes.

This super vegetable has a phytochemical called lycopene that prevents the growth of cancer cells. They are high in antioxidants and vitamins to prevent age-related illnesses. They have healthy acids to facilitate breaking down of glucose to transform into energy and help diabetic patients as well. Choline is also one of its nutrients responsible for keeping our cells and muscles healthy. It is proven to contain healthy omega-3 acids that is a recipe for a healthy heart. Furthermore, as if it could not get any better than this, tomatoes also contain folic acid that prevents the production of a certain brain chemical that is responsible for feelings of depression. Hence, not only do tomatoes keep us healthy, but they also keep us happy and energized.

The best way of growing tomatoes is to use large pots. So, you can allocate at least a square foot of space for this plant, then you can place a stake or cage around it to contain the leaves from taking up more space. You will need something that is about 18 centimeters in height to accommodate the roots of the tomato plant. If you have access to it, place a small fiberglass screen at the bottom of your pot to prevent the soil from draining along with your water. A saucer will also help in draining the water more thoroughly, these usually come with purchased pots. Expect this tomato plant to be heavy which will hinder your mobility, hence it would be better to use plastic pots to reduce the weight and just make sure to put the plant in a place where it could get enough sun exposure throughout the day.

3. Cucumbers

Cucumbers or scientifically known as *cucumis sativus* are one of the highly cultivated plants in the world. And why not? They have very low calorie content and they don't have any cholesterol. They are good for your diet because they contain fiber that cleanses your colon and reduces constipation. Moreover, these veggies are high in potassium, anti-oxidants, vitamins A, B, C, and K, so they reduce high blood pressure and facilitates bone growth. There are several varieties that you can choose as well, like Northern Cucumber, Bush Pickle, and Lemon Cucumbers.

Cucumbers are better grown in a raised bed with a frame or trellis around the bed as cucumbers grow in vines. If you are starting from seeds be sure to wait for 2 weeks after the last winter frost to make sure that the soil is warm enough for the seeds to germinate. If you are transplanting, make sure to keep the seeds in house under warm light bulbs.

When you plant them, dig a hole on the soil about half to an inch deep. Drop 5 to 8 seeds in the soil, this will increase your chance of success, but you may have to transfer some later on. Then, softly cover the seeds with soil but do not pat or squish the soil in place, it will damage the seeds. If you are transplanting, be very careful in handling the seedling. Make sure that the soil is hard enough so as not to damage the roots and then plant them a foot a part from each other.

Once you've planted the seeds and seedlings, water your plants gradually. Do not oversaturate the pot or bed, make sure that the water flows to the bottom and drops from the drainage holes. Cucumbers require moist soil to grow and to check for the moisture content, stick your finger up to your knuckles and if your fingertip comes out wet, then your moisture levels are okay. If it's dry, water slowly and gradually to make sure that the soil is actually absorbing it.

Add organic fertilizers once a week to help maintain the moisture and keep the plant healthy. Use water soluble and organic fertilizers if possible. Also, be sure to protect your cucumber from the wind, especially during spring time. It is best to place them against a wall or against a fence. Neem oil is an effective pesticide and it's natural so it is safe to use with your veggie.

Cucumbers are fast-growing veggies so expect some fruits within a few weeks, about 50 to 70 days. Harvest cucumbers while they still look young and within a small to medium sized. Cucumbers get bitter as they age.

4. Herbs

You can plant these fresh and aromatic herbs along with your vegetables or you can place them in one container. These are very compact and you can replant them simply by cutting a stem diagonally and sticking it to the soil, except for Rosemary. The container should be 8 to 10 inches deep and you can have 2 to 3 herbs per square inch. All of these thrive in hot and dry conditions so make sure that they are exposed to sunlight, but keep the soil moisturized, especially with basil and stevia.

- Oregano
- Rosemary
- Sage
- Tarragon
- Thyme
- Marjoram
- Basil
- Stevia

PLANTS BEST SERVED COLD

1. Cauliflower

This beautiful, flower vegetable has been titled as a superfood. And it is no wonder because it contains, dietary fibers, antioxidants, anti-inflammatory nutrients, phytonutrients, choline, vitamins and minerals, and nutrients that fight against cancer, hypertension, and kidney problems.

This cruciferous vegetable should be planted in the 2 to 3 month mark after the last frost of the winter season or at the end of the late spring or summer seasons. Cauliflowers require pots like that of the tomatoes, 12 inches deep and 12 inches in diameter. For cold season plants, it is preferable to use transplants or seedlings.

Fill your container with soil until an inch before the rim. Make a hole in the center enough to fit a seedling's roots or a smaller one for seeds. If you have seedlings, softly remove them from the nursery pots by squeezing both sides until the plant slides out then use the other hand to gently place the plant into the pot. For seeds, place at most four seeds in the hole. Then, gently cover with soil and water to keep it moisturized. Put in ph-balanced water soluble fertilizer.

Place the container outside one month before winter season and make sure that it is exposed to sunlight. You can place your pot on your balcony or on a raised area for maximum coolness. Always keep the soil moisturized, NEVER let it dry out.

Blanche your cauliflowers when its diameter reaches 2 to 3 inches. You will notice that its color green, but you can turn it white by covering the head with its own leaves tied together at the top. The optimal diameter for harvesting is 7 inches or around 3 to 4 months (for transplants), and harvest your cauliflower by using a sharp knife in cutting below the head low enough that you include the leaves with your harvest. Do not reuse the soil to put in other plants because you are putting future plants at higher risk of diseases.

This process of planting is also applicable to other cruciferous plants, such as broccoli, cabbage, kale, and turnips.

2. Spinach

Probably every kid hates spinach and every parent who wants to keep their child healthy, force feeds this to them. But, if you involve your children in planting and harvesting this plant then there is a higher chance that in the next meal there would be less resistance to eating the vegetables. This is also Popeye's famous source of superpower because truly if you have this in your garden, you'll start feeling as strong as Popeye. This vegetable contains, iron, calcium, potassium, and phosphorous all involved in muscle and bone building. It also contains Vitamins A, C, E, and K and

B6 for brain health. Folate, one of the nutrients in spinach, helps your cardiovascular system. And the magnesium keeps your blood pressure at a healthy level. If you trained your kids or yourself to eat vegetables like this regularly, then not only would you save money from growing your own food but also on medications.

Spinach can be planted in your raised bed that's only 8 to 10 inches deep. You can plant them in a row 30 centimeters apart from each other. When using seedlings, handle the roots carefully because they are very fine and fibrous so they can tear very easily.

Watering should be your number one priority with this plant, their leaves need to be kept moisturized and so do the soil. Fish emulsions or compost tea are recommended to use in place of fertilizers for better yields.

Also, you need to watch out for pests and worms. As spinach is a leafy vegetables it can attract a lot of worms and insects and they will use the leaves as nests for their larvae. Pick off the leaves whose undersides have white streaks of larvae. You can use garlic soap spray to remove them or spinosad, an organic antibacterial implement, to prevent further pests from attacking.

You can harvest your spinach leaves in less than a month, easy! You can use this same planting process for lettuces as well.

3. Carrots

Carrots are a big source of Vitamin A, Vitamin C, calcium, fiber, carotene, zinc, manganese, fiber, folate, and other essential vitamins and minerals. When you eat at least half a cup of carrots every day, you would not be needing those vitamin capsules anymore. Or you can make a carrot shake or smoothie to make swallowing easier.

Carrots can also come in different colors like yellow, red, and purple. Each purple has a unique antioxidant which is also the cause for their unique colors. You can ask for seeds or seedlings of these unique carrot species from the farmer's market.

Raised beds and deep pots are best for growing carrots and other root crops. Anything with a depth of more than 12 inches is enough for carrots. You can plant several seeds, up to 4 seeds in every one inch squares, that's a lot for one pot or raised bed. However, carrot seeds are tiny and you may lose control with how many you put in one area. So, just let them grow before thinning or cutting out the smaller leaves to allow the stronger ones to grow. Like other cold weather plants, the soil needs to always be moisturized. Never allow the surface to dry. They also prefer loose or loamier soil.

Within 2 weeks your carrots will have already sprouted, they are quite sensitive to changing weather conditions so it would help if you can place them somewhere it could get enough breeze and sunlight. Optimum temperature is at 13 degrees Celsius. And voila, in just 2 to

2 and a half months, you will have your homegrown carrots on your plates! Harvest them by grasping the leafy tops and gently wiggling them out of the soil. The younger the carrots, the sweeter they will be.

The same planting methods could be applied to other root crops such as beets, potatoes, and radishes.

4. Onions

As we all know, onions are like tomatoes. They are necessary to making your food taste great. These are one of the plants in which you could use all of its part for food, both the bulb and the leaves. This is a very low maintenance and very fast-growing plant. You can plant multiple seeds in one pot or bottle container and you can just snip the leaves and let it grow for very long periods of time.

Onions can practically grow in any container, but the cheapest way is to plant them in the plastic bottles. As for the soil, it will need a loamy soil enriched with compost. The faster way to grow onions is to use transplants or alive bulbs. Place one bulb per 3-inch square of the container. Bury them just into the soil until where the green color starts from the bulb. Onions require little care and maintenance, only a cooler temperature and moist soil. If you want to fertilize, feed your onions with compost tea.

If you want to harvest the bulbs, you will have to wait until the tops start to yellow and droop. When this happens, you should bend the tops down further to stop the ripening. You'll have to wait again for the tops to turn brown before you can pull the onion bulb, always be careful when doing this because the bulbs might bruise and rot. As the soil is moist, lay your bulbs to dry before using them. As for the green onions, you may trim the leaves when the plant has reached 6 to 8 inches tall.

5. Herbs

If there are herbs that thrive in dry climate, these herbs grow in cold climate conditions. They will produce flowers and seeds in the summer but their leaves will turn bitter which is not good for your food.

- Parsley
- Coriander
- Dill
- Cilantro

Chapter 6 - Gardening TLC Lessons

Gardening is not just about plants and containers, there are many other factors that makes a plant grow, such as soil, weather, and the gardener himself. Hence, here are some things you need to know about taking care of your plants.

I. Soil and fertilizer ingredients

Your plants won't grow without soil, but it also won't grow with just plain old soil that we often see on the ground. The soil have to be a mixture of nutrients, specifically potassium, phosphorous, and nitrogen, that is conducive for planting. Microorganisms are working together to release the necessary nutrients that'll keep your plant alive and growing. What is often used in gardening today are soil mixes which are a combination of organic and minerals that aids water flow, airflow, decontamination, and nutrition. Some of the ingredients in a typical soil mix are:

- Organic matter or decomposed matter: they provide the microorganisms for plant nutrition and health

- Limestone: this regulates the pH levels of the soil and provides calcium and magnesium to the plants.

- Sand: aids water flow

- Peat moss: retains water to keep soil moisturized as well as improving drainage.

- Vermiculite: mineral flakes that expands to help in aerating and water flowing in the soil

Fertilizers are the ones that contain the nitrogen, phosphorous, and potassium (N-P-K). Each plant has different nutritional needs, so when you purchase your fertilizer make sure to understand what your plant needs and read the label of the fertilizer. The label should provide you with three numbers which indicate the amount of N-P-K there is for each mix. Even though organic fertilizers can be more expensive, they are still preferable because they do not just provide NPK, they also provide other micronutrients and they are less likely to damage the soil and the plant roots.

II. Natural insecticides and pesticides

When you start your garden, expect to have other species involved other than plants. This is a natural occurrence and not something you should be afraid of, but it has to be controlled otherwise only these pests will benefit from your plants.

There is a method in gardening which is called the "three sisters garden" where you can arrange certain plants in one container because they help each other grow. Similarly, you can use one plant's defense mechanism to protect the other plants. There are plants who have a natural ability to deter certain types of pests, so what you can do is surround that plant along the plant who attracts the pests.

Also, you can use biological controls or living organisms to fight against the living organisms attacking your plants. Some of these biological controls are spinosad, nematodes, milky spores, and Bt. You can also use natural oils instead of spraying chemical pesticides, like neem oil, garlic oil, pyrethrins, summer oils that are plant friendly, and insecticidal soaps. These may be available at your gardening shops.

CONCLUSION

Thank you again for downloading this book!

Congratulations! You now have the solution in your hands. It is up to you to put it into action. You have learned how important plants are into our lives and how gardening will improve the way we live. More than that, you have been provided with concrete steps into making all these come to life through urban gardening.

So, start your own garden now! Bring out your creativity, your resourcefulness, your commitment, and your compassion for the world. Take a step towards making a change and challenge people's way of living by starting your own way through sustainable living. Start with growing your own food and become more self-reliant.

Because now you can start to imagine the world becoming a better place and the TV sharing more good news than bad. Let us start living meaningful lives, rebuilding relationships, and reconnecting with nature through urban gardening.

Finally, if you enjoyed this book, then I'd like to ask you for a favor, would you be kind enough to leave a review for this book on Amazon? It'd be greatly appreciated!

Click here to leave a review for this book on Amazon!

Thank you and good luck!

Made in the USA
Columbia, SC
06 April 2018